100 Ways

TO

Declutter

YOUR HOME

FIONA FERRIS

Dear lovely reader,

Perhaps, like me, you have read a lot of different organizing, tidying, decluttering, and simple living books. You have dutifully followed the 'easy steps' in articles on how to streamline your home.

You love having your favourite things around you, but you don't love feeling suffocated by stuff. You adore your favourite books, creature comforts, and abundance of pretty goodies, but also dream of living a divinely minimal life where everything is easy, and you could go off on a long trip at a moment's notice.

You know you're not a hoarder, and your home looks reasonable to most people, but you feel the need to go further. You want to streamline *everything* and have it stay that way. You no longer want to second guess whether to keep something or donate it.

This is me, and maybe it's you too. People who know me say I am organized, tidy and neat. They look around my home and say, 'I don't see anything that needs decluttering'. And it's true, I have done a lot of work over the years and made many sifts of my possessions.

But some of us are *stickier* than others. We get a handle on one category and another springs up in its place. It almost seems like a different person did all the buying and collecting! But when we are in the moment and want that thing, it is the most natural choice in the world to purchase it.

I know. It's exhausting!

We already know the practical steps to simplifying our space, of course we do, it's simple, isn't it? Put things in a box and remove them from our home. But sometimes we can get bogged down. Sometimes we need a little inspiration. And when the right message hits us at the right time, that's when we can take off and *fly*.

That's what I offer you in this book. One hundred tips to inspire you, encourage you, and yes, persuade you to part with things you don't necessarily believe are adding to your life, yet have resistance towards getting rid of.

If we could just see what's on the other side, none of this would be an issue! When we know what is awaiting us over the rainbow, we can't wait to get started. That's why I love working on my mindset, it makes everything easier. When we flick the switch in our mind, things change for the better, and with no effort either. It's almost like a miracle when it happens.

Please take this mini-book in the relaxed spirit it is offered: as a down-to-earth (yet fanciful) guide and mentor. You will find motivation when you need it, and a friendly encouraging hand.

Flip through and find something that resonates, or take a few hours and read the whole lot at once. Become so fired up that your new obsession is decluttering and tidying instead of those other... less helpful... obsessions such as gossipy scrolling, online shopping, and eating for fun. Yes, those are some of mine!

Life is too short to spend surrounded by clutter and junk. It's too short to feel like we're not winning every day. So join me in the pages of *100 Ways to Declutter Your Home* and let's make magic together. Let's create our dream home: one day, one decision, and one action at a time. Wouldn't you love to live in *your dream home*? Me too! Let's get on with it!

I hope you love this book and get *loads* of useful nuggets from it. Now let's get straight into one-hundred ways to declutter your home, in a fun, easy, exciting, and light-hearted way. Exciting!

With warmest regards from a rainy and cozy winter's day in Hawke's Bay, New Zealand,

100 Ways to Declutter Your Home

1. **Reframe decluttering for yourself**. Instead of thinking about everything you are 'throwing out', 'wasting', and 'getting rid of', and dithering over things you might need one day, consider this. Living in a tidy, streamlined, and organized home, means you are *choosing the present* and showing yourself and others that having a peaceful environment is your highest priority. *Choose a peaceful, serene existence*. Remember the past with fondness, and look forward to a beautiful future, but give yourself the gift of the present, just like the poem says. It really is the best place to live.

2. **Start with a vision**. It might be a feeling you have for your home, or perhaps a style for just

one room. Maybe you want to make your bedroom feel more feminine, peaceful, and relaxing. So, you would remove everything that does *not* promote those feelings which delight your feminine being: your stationary exercise bike, the clothes basket, a teetering stack of books... And add in things that do: soft colours and textures, giving your bedroom a complete spring clean, changing the bedding, curating your bedside table to display only a few items such as a book, pretty hand cream, and lamp. If you desire to makeover your whole home, close your eyes and imagine how your ideal lifestyle would look and feel. Use this as your filter as you start to declutter and organize.

3.   **See what is getting in the way** between you and your ideal life. Mentally step through your entire house and make a note of the areas that are bothersome to you; those areas which *aren't* supporting your vision. Perhaps your closet needs sorting with the change of season. Or your craft area has become a dumping ground for anything that needs a temporary home. Find storage areas which haven't been sorted in a long time (or ever: I found a few in our home and we've lived here five years). Make a master list of everything that is blocking you from the beautiful vision you have for your home, and work through it. Start

with the most annoying one first, or the easiest just to get you going. The most important thing is that you make a start.

4. **Stop buying stuff**. When you buy something, it costs money. Then you have to find a place to put it. And time to look after it. You have to insure it, clean it, and 'manage' it. This all takes energy. So put the brakes on what is coming into your home and give yourself a chance to catch up with what you have. Take the time to figure out what you're going to do with the things that are cluttering up your space. Often buying something new is just a habit, so in the interim, perhaps purchase something small in price and consumable if you feel the need to buy a treat, such as a barista coffee or single-serve higher quality chocolate bar. My favourite if I'm out and want to get myself something is a Whittaker's 33% Creamy Milk bar (the 50g size).

5. **Commit to using things up**. You will have areas that you habitually over-purchase in, I certainly do. Mine are candles, books and magazines, cosmetics, body products, and perfume. Yours might be different. I used to know a girl who bought a new pair of (inexpensive) sunglasses just about every single week! It was her 'thing'. Anyway,

whatever *your* areas are, firstly identify them, and then commit to using up the stock you already have. I no longer buy magazines and have cut down drastically on books. I am not buying body lotion *no matter how pretty it smells*, and the same with makeup and perfume, until I have actually run out of something. It's been fun shopping my own stash, and so satisfying to finish something up and move onto the next product. It gives me the same high as shopping, it's free, *and* I get to declutter my bathroom – yay!

6.   **'Empty' your fridge**. Seeing a clean, shiny, brightly lit, almost empty fridge makes me feel so happy! And it's because I have gotten rid of the clutter in there: the half-used jar of green curry paste that I've not used in a long time and now no longer want to. The piece of cheese that I left too long (I am not with the French on stinky cheeses). The jar of pâté I was given, and we opened it but never used again because I don't like pâté and it seems my husband doesn't either. I don't like to waste food, but I gave myself permission to have a big clean out. I then wiped down all the shelves and put back everything that made the cut. It is such a wonderful feeling to be greeted by a fridge that is clean, bright, and inviting. The angels really do sing when I open my fridge door now. And

it's satisfying to have used everything up and start fresh with a new week of groceries.

7. **Eat from your freezer**. Many people I know, me included at one stage, have overflowing freezers. We put purchases and leftovers in there and it can be quite some time before we ever see them again if we don't check the freezer for meal options. Take an inventory. See how many bags of frozen vegetables you have, how many parcels of meat, how many takeout alternatives such as frozen fries and pizza, and how many freezer meals you've made. Make yourself a big list and commit to *eating your stock*. Just as with an overstocked fridge or pantry, a too-full freezer makes it difficult to remember what you have in there. Frozen food doesn't last forever. And if you don't fancy eating it, throw it out. Give yourself permission to get rid of food that no longer looks good. Start afresh and commit to keeping your freezer inventory rotated regularly.

8. **Choose to live in a home not a warehouse**. When you store lots and have trouble letting it go, you are by default living in a warehouse, where you have every conceivable item available to you instantly. This sounds like a handy situation to be in, but your home has its limits, and you may well

have reached yours. Instead, why not choose to leave all those extra goods at the store, where they will still be readily available to you, but that you don't have to purchase and manage before you might need them one day. This one thought alone has helped me lower my grocery spending, which as we all know is a welcome outcome with grocery prices these days. I shop once a week, and only purchase what I need for the next seven days. It took some practice not to stock up, especially after the pandemic, but now it's a fun game to see how little I can buy. Try it, and I'm sure you will become hooked as well!

9. **Find your rewards**. Decluttering and organizing your home is not just drudgery that never ends, where you have to wrench precious items away from yourself and give them away. I know that's how many people see it, and when my mind is not in the right mood, I can feel like that too. But *look at the rewards*. Consider what you will do with your time when you're not feeling overwhelmed looking for something you need or sorting out your messy house once again. When you're not spending that extra daily time sorting through your clothes finding something to wear or hours on the weekend tidying your garage or spare room, you will have time to sew and craft, go for a sunny stroll, or read a book in a café. You

will be able to do all these things *without guilt*, because you have the time. You have committed to making all the categories in your home as efficient as they can be, and now you are reaping the rewards. Write down all the things you are going to do 'one day' when your house is in order and you have all this free time. Use this list as your motivation as you sort through your home.

10. **Move as quickly as you can**. This is my secret success tip that I use for anything I want to achieve, whether it's tidying up the house, prepping dinner, or writing a chapter. I'm not saying to go fast and make mistakes, but to move briskly and economically. Don't start reading books as you go through them! You can decide if you want to keep or donate a book by holding it, looking at the cover, and taking a few seconds to flick through it. Set a timer on your phone and tell yourself that you're going to go through your bookshelf in twenty minutes and come up with ten books to declutter. Or that you have fifteen minutes to choose your very favourite clothes from your closet (and then consider why the others didn't make the cut). Whatever task you choose, *move quickly*. Confident action ignites purpose in your brain and you will be happy with the results, I promise.

11. **Stop watching television**, or at least cut back. This only has to be temporary if you want, but what I have found is that having the television on *sucks up time*. Time that you could use to move forward with your life! And the computer screen is the same. I don't often turn the television on until after dinner, but I do browse around on the internet during the day which I consider the same thing. When I turn my computer off at a certain time (when I have finished my book writing for the day, for example) and tell myself I can't turn it on again until tomorrow, it's amazing how much I get done. I actually go looking for things to do. There's a fabulous phrase that says, 'When you do things, things get done', and it's true. So, turn your screen off and *make tracks*.

12. **The onion method**. You may have heard of it, and thankfully it's *very* straightforward. It is a method of decluttering where you simply go layer by layer. The first layer, whether it's of a category or your complete home, will yield good results. And then after you let things settle, you go through that same category again (another layer) and streamline some more. You will always find you can go a little further each time. It is a good method to use if you are intimidated by 'the big clear out'. For some, having a huge clean-up is motivating, but for many of us we are scared to make mistakes.

We need a gentler approach. I have used the onion method for many years, and it has brought me a home of order, peace and tranquility. And, every so often when I find the inventory creeping up, I'll use the onion method again. It will never fail you!

13. **Get that good feeling for yourself**. When you visit someone who has a home that is clean, decluttered and organized, it always feels good to be there. There might not be anything particularly special about where they live, but it's how they care for their possessions that makes it feel that way. Likely their closet is orderly too, and not crammed with unused clothes. Their car is probably the same way. It might be a basic, used car, but see how pristine they keep it and how it's cleaned out after a trip. Everything goes together – the house, the car, the wardrobe. For these people, taking care of their belongings is a non-negotiable and it makes ordinary spaces seem extraordinary. When you get into habits like this, you will make an impression on people and they will never forget it. And you win most of all, because you get to live with the results every day of your life.

14. **The question to ask of your books**. I used to have a lot of books, and kept just about every book I'd ever bought. I did this because I told

myself I loved books! Then one day I had an epiphany. We'd just moved house, it was a rental, and it was tiny. I was trying to unpack my books and find space for them. I was getting overwhelmed because there wasn't enough room for all my books. My epiphany was that many of my books didn't interest me enough to read, even if they were sitting on a library shelf available to borrow for free, let alone pay full retail. It was quite disheartening as I looked at all the money I had spent. But keeping them wasn't getting any of my money back, so that day I sat down, went through every book and asked myself, *Would I borrow this from the library today?* If the answer was no, I put it in a box. These days I would just donate them to a thrift store, but back then we were saving for our first home and I also thought my books were worth something. So, I took boxes and boxes along to a second-hand bookstore and was dismayed when they offered me only $1 or $2 each for the books they wanted to buy. Books that still looked brand new which I had paid $25-$30 each for! This experience has stayed with me, and definitely made me more intentional with any future book purchases. And these days I have regular cleanouts to keep my collection manageable and current. When I do this, the books I keep are more precious. They are fun to flick through because I have a curated collection right there on the bookshelf in the hall. Not stacked in boxes in a cupboard somewhere because they don't all fit on my bookshelves!

15. **Let a collection lay unfinished**. Collections are *such a hard thing to resist* for some of us. We want the whole set! That's how I ended up with an English China Whimsies ornament collection as a young girl. And every issue of my favourite English 'Girl' magazine. And all the Sweet Valley High books. And in current times many bottles of fragrance because another 'flanker' was released of one of my favourites. Or a set of Penny Vincenzi books. I have enjoyed a few of her books and thought it would be a good idea to collect them inexpensively for future reading. I looked out for them anytime I was passing a thrift store or second-hand bookshop. But then what did I do? Only moved on to another author! I will go back to Penny eventually, but in the meantime, I have eight of her books taking up valuable real estate on my home library shelf. And I could have just as easily borrowed them from the public library one at a time! Now when I feel the collection frenzy feeling come on, I say to myself, *It's okay to have an incomplete collection; it's okay to stop now*. And it's okay for you too.

16. **Take a before photo and get moving**. One day I walked into my kitchen, and it looked like a bombsite. Not so much with dishes, they were in the dishwasher, but I had bits and pieces strewn everywhere. There were random items on the counter, like the blender I wanted to donate. It had been there over a week and annoyed me every time I saw it. There was also a newspaper I'd bought because it had an article featuring my brother, so I started by putting that into my family mementos box (a wooden box the size of a large shoebox). But before I started, I decided to be my own television home makeover host and took a quick photo with my phone so I could do a before-and-after *ta da* for myself. In less than half an hour my kitchen was transformed with this mini tidying session. I felt on top of the world, but the part that gave me the most oomph was looking forward to comparing my before and after photos. Let me tell you, the sense of satisfaction as I flicked between these two photos was immense! *And* I was rewarded with a tidy kitchen. I can thoroughly recommend the photo technique as fun motivation for a problem spot you feel stuck in.

17. **Tidy your space to tidy your diet**. I mostly have healthy eating habits with plenty of vegetables and not too many snacks. But every

so often I become less interested in my nutritious regime, and more interested in chocolate, popcorn, and ice cream. At these times *they call my name*. It's only recently that I made the connection between junk food cravings and a cluttered home. When my home becomes messy, my thinking gets messy too! As soon as I click to this I make an effort to tidy areas and it puts me back into a good space again – both mentally *and* physically! It really does feel like peeling off the cluttery layers of my home helps peel the cluttery layers off my body. As soon as you start decluttering and tidying you will feel lighter and freer, and you will find it easier to be intentional with your eating and drinking when you are simplifying your home.

18. **Become *dynamic*.** Claim this word as motivational fuel when you need it. But be gentle on yourself; choose to be *softly dynamic*. A leaning-back, feminine flavour of dynamic. This translates to being self-motivated, energized, efficient, productive, progressive, peppy and zippy. Doesn't this sound amazing? You are not charging ahead at full speed unaware of what's around you. Rather, you are taking effective action. You are focused and driven. You are lively. You get things done because you are self-propelling. You are energizing to be around. Your days are

productive in a relaxed and efficient way. You make progress towards your ideal life every day, even if nothing big is achieved. It's just that you are living that day as you see your future days unfolding and it feels wonderful. So claim being the measured and calm, softly dynamic woman as your focus.

19. **Ask your future self to inspire you**. Perhaps you have this dreamy vision of the future you that pops into your mind every so often. I see mine living in a buzzy, beachside townhouse or apartment, very compact and minimal. It's her base to come and go from as she visits and travels, and her zen sanctuary when she is at home. She is healthy, vital and happy. It's a wonderful vision to have, try it for yourself! Close your eyes and think about your future self and see what comes to you. Then, ask her how she came to be in this place? Ask her how she created this reality for herself? When I asked my future self this in a quiet meditation one day, she told me: *I chose an elegant life. I chose peace and harmony. I chose simplicity. I chose to please myself. I chose my own point of view. I chose me.* And her advice to me was: *Choose you.* It actually gave me chills! Try asking your future self what advice she has for you. It's a fun little meander, and the other cool thing is that you will feel

very peaceful and serene after a session with your lovely future self!

20. **'Haven't you paid enough?'** I heard this phrase in relation to excuses and objections when it comes to decluttering, and it's very helpful in countering the sticky thought of, 'I paid a lot for that, I can't just give it away'. Depending on the item and your budget, 'a lot' can be $2, $50 or $2,000. It's not the amount that trips us up, but the thought. Sadly, the money is gone, whether we keep the item or not. We have already spent the money, and unless we sell the item we won't be getting any of it back. (And we are highly unlikely to receive the amount we paid for it if we do sell it.) In the meantime we are paying over and over again – with time, attention, and emotion. Whether you keep something forever or donate it, no money will be returned to your account. The money left when you spent it. You simply cannot redeem a purchase by keeping that item! Really, haven't you paid enough? The money is gone, the exchange happened, but we keep paying with low-vibe feelings over and over. It's time to let ourselves off the hook. Keep this question for when you need it: *Haven't I paid enough?*

21. **When you hold onto smaller size clothes**. Do you have a guest closet with

smaller size clothes in it? Yeah, me too. And I was always looking for a good mindset shift to make it easy for me to clean out this collection in its entirety! The 'Haven't you paid enough?' reframe is so apt in this situation. For those of us who have gained weight, we are torturing and taunting ourselves by keeping these clothes around – sometimes for *years*. Punishing ourselves, and for what? Changing shape? Such a crime! But imagine if you did get back to that ideal weight you have in your mind. Wouldn't you gain immense pleasure from going out and buying new clothes? Of course, it would be amazingly fun! And that could be the gift waiting for you if your weight changes, not digging through several-years-old clothes to see what will fit you. Mmmm, what a prize you can't wait to win! Such an enticement! Really, what's exciting about rummaging through bins of old clothes to find something that fits, but that you no longer like? There is no reward in that at all. Let the clothes go, move forward freely, and relish the empty space in your guest closet.

22. **The smaller-size project**. Perhaps we aren't ready to let go of all of our smaller-size clothes just yet. We have many good reasons for keeping them. They cost us money and yes, that's money gone, but we love most of the pieces. When we wore them we looked great

and *felt really good in them*. We received compliments on our outfits and how we looked. So what if you give it your best shot this year to fit them? And whatever doesn't fit, you're donating. Or sell if you can find a good way to, but whatever, by this date next year you are going to fit everything you own one way or another. Give yourself a deadline and make it a fun focus. Operation Wardrobe!

23. **An excellent clothes decluttering question**. When you are standing in front of your closet wondering what to do about all your extra clothes, ask yourself this question: *If I fit this and it was the correct season, would I want to wear it right now?* And, if you don't want to theoretically wear it, it goes into the donate pile (or a 'cooling off' box that you will donate on a certain date in the future). Some items won't excite you anymore, some will bore you, some will have weird feelings attached to them and so on. Give yourself the freedom to only keep an item if you really, really like it. Because if you don't even like it anymore, what is the point of owning it? Considering the question: *If I fit this and it was the correct season, would I want to wear it right now?* helped me easily clear out almost half of my clothes that I'd been keeping for a while but not wearing. It felt so good, and I didn't even feel deprived. You don't have to

wait for the correct season or to have lost any weight either. It's instant gratification!

24. **Choose a highly simplified life**. Do you adore gazing at staged real estate listings or deliciously minimal and tidy Airbnb images? Me too! There is no excess or clutter, just neat vistas and exactly what you would need for a pleasing living environment, nothing extra. Many of us no longer want tons of stuff, things for 'just in case', items which we store but never use or display, or the general feeling of being bogged down. But it's a big step to really pare down to the beautiful and the essential. So what's holding us back? For me, I know it is because I neatly store things. All my clutter is tucked away in storage containers. Even tidily stowed items can silently nag us though, because they are still in our home. But we put them there in the first place! And, we can let them go. There is peace in that. We are the ones in charge. And we have permission to only have what we want in our home.

25. **The dinner perspective**. Like me, you probably buy dinner out sometimes. It might be delicious and a lovely evening, or maybe not such a good experience. Not every restaurant visit will be a winner, but we eat the meal, pay our money and go home. We chose to spend that money, we had the meal, and then it was

finished. With clothing and other items, we buy the piece and take it home. Maybe we wear or use it a lot or maybe it doesn't quite live up to the expectation we had for it. But do we pass it along? No! And often the price point is lower than a meal out which we happily move on from once that evening has passed. It is the *permanent physicalness* of the item bought that trips many of us up. We don't carry around the purchase price of a meal for years, but we do with purchases. So the next time you are hesitating over donating an item that you no longer want but can't seem to let go of, remember the dinner perspective. You can have enjoyed (or learned from) your purchase and let it move on.

26.   **The money-back filter**. If you were offered your money back, right now, for a particular item in your home, would you take it and hand over that item gladly? And would you feel nothing but relief? If so, this in itself tells you that particular item is adding nothing to your life (and is in fact detracting), because there are many things you own that you wouldn't give up even if you could be given the cash right now. The next question is what are you going to do with it? Are you going to use it up and not repurchase? Donate? Sell? Whatever you choose, let the next step be *towards your peace of mind*. Remember, you never signed a

contract that said you promised to keep everything you ever bought forever. You are free to let go of anything in your life. Let the money-back filter identify those items for you.

27. **Mining for gold**. I often have the word 'sifting' in my head when I am decluttering. In a similar way to the onion method where you peel back layers, sifting involves more than one go too. The first sift yields good returns, and then each subsequent sift refines that area or category even further. What you may not have been able to let go of the first time, you might in the second. The gold and gems are uncovered and you remember why you loved them, or even that you still own them. You get to enjoy what you have kept because it is not buried under all the other rubbish. Items actually look newer and more appealing when they are lifted out on their own after the rest is taken away. You like them more, are inspired to care for them better, and they seem to blossom under your sunshine. This has happened so often for me and it never fails to dazzle me with the magic of it. When you declutter, you really *are* mining for gold. Go and find yours! It's waiting in your home to be discovered!

28. **Find a local auction house**. If you are a happy online seller, great. I used to do this

back in the day, but these days it just seems like a big hassle to me, plus we live in the country now so it's not convenient for people to come and pick things up that aren't suitable to post. Then I found out about a local auction house that sells household goods. I had a few items that seemed 'too good' to donate and they just sat in a cupboard taking up space. I had a few Nao figurines (Lladro apprentices do them) that my nana had given me a long time ago but aren't really my style. I used to use them in tablescapes but hadn't in ages. So I sent them along to the auction along with a bowl of crystals I bought twenty years ago when I was going through a crystal phase, a silver hip flask my husband was given for his 21st (I checked with him first!), and a few other things like that. I received $150 for the lot, *and* I freed up space. $150 cash for things that I didn't really know how to get rid of! I was so happy! Auctions are great for these kinds of items, so see if there is one in your town.

29. **Question everything in your possession**, even if you have skipped over it in the past. Ask yourself, 'Do I really like this, or has it been in my life so long that I don't even notice it's there anymore? And does it still represent who I am?' Those are the questions to run through your mind. Do I really want all these crochet patterns when I haven't had the desire to

crochet in years? Do I want all these baby patterns for clothing and toys when no-one I know is having babies and if they did, I'd probably buy them a gift rather than make one? When everything is on probation, even long-standing hobbies and items, it is *liberating*.

30. **How to lose the guilt when decluttering**? For me, it's gifts I have been given, or items that someone has passed on to me that they've bought but then wanted to declutter. I have kept items only because I know the person who gave them to me would be disappointed if I didn't. This doesn't sound like a very good reason when I write it out, I can see that now! Life is simply too short to store goods like this. Guilt is not a valid reason to keep something! But in truth I have thought to myself occasionally, 'I am going to have to keep this item until X dies one day.' Well, no more. Have you arrived at the same point as me? Sure, you may display (or wear) that item for a while, but ultimately you are the one who gets to decide what happens to it. If someone gave it to you, you can give it away. Others can't control what happens to something once it is in your house! This is an important distinction that many of us can forget. We don't want to seem mean or cold-hearted, and with a few items that might be fine, but not with everything, otherwise

we'd be crowded out of our house. *We* get to choose what we keep and what we discard. Imagine only keeping the things that make you feel amazing, wouldn't that be the best way to live?

31. **Clean out your knicker drawer**! If you're at home reading this, go to your underwear drawer and count how many pairs you have. I had *tons*. I counted at least forty pairs! And of course I wore my favourite, most comfortable ones all the time and ignored the others. What helped me do a satisfying cleanout was the question: *If someone was doing my washing because I was unwell, or if I died tomorrow and people cleaned out my stuff, would they look at my underwear and think how sad it was that I wore stretched-out old-looking bras and past-their-best knickers?* I actually held each pair of knickers up to see if they qualified as 'sad'. My favourites that I'd had for a while did, so they were binned. I kept newer favourites. I also took out all the pairs that I just didn't like. The lace was scratchy, the straps were too skinny and cut in. I don't like boyleg cut. I more than halved my pairage and now have a much smaller selection that all make me smile. Each pair I enjoy wearing and none are sad! When you do this too you will feel so happy getting dressed every day!

32. **Self-discovery *par excellence***. I don't know about you, but when I spend time decluttering and organizing, I find out more about myself. I find out what the real treasures are, and what lights me up. Decluttering leading to self-discovery is a real thing! You can see, quite literally often, the next version of yourself. Sometimes you will have hung onto things such as clothing because you used to love it and think you will again, but then you don't want to wear it. That piece doesn't feel like 'you' anymore when you put it on. It's a funny thing to experience, when you can feel yourself accelerating past your old self. It definitely feels like you are moving quickly. It's actually a thrilling prospect: like the ultimate project to craft the future you. It's a brand-new canvas to splash with art in any style you like. Let yourself go forward to discover the next version of you.

33. **Move freely through life**. When you keep your home in a simplified and organized state, you get to advance easily and fluidly through your years. Why not plan to be more flexible and open to change as the years go by, instead of becoming more rigid and set in your ways (which is what most people do)? Doesn't it sound more enjoyable to stay loose and limber in your mind than slowly settling into premature rigor mortis? And what I love about

using things up, sorting out stuff to donate, and tidying the things I love and have kept, is that shopping for more stuff has never seemed less appealing. It's a strange fact that when you are drowning in clutter you shop for more, and when you are cleaning it out you don't desire to shop at all unless it's for something absolutely necessary. There is no need to understand how it works in your mind because you can feel for yourself that it's the truth!

34. **Find yourself some motivating viewing**. I have a few personal favourites when I want to get going but need a little push. Peter Walsh, decluttering guru, author of several excellent books and famous for being on the Oprah show is fabulous. He is so down-to-earth and practical. You could read one of his books or find some clips of him on YouTube. Anthea Turner is another favourite. She had a show called 'Perfect Housewife' in the UK which I have on DVD. I watch an episode when I need a boost and it always works. It doesn't matter the flavour of your personal motivational favourites, just that you find what rings *your* bell, and use them when necessary. They can be the match to ignite your flame!

35. **Lighten your spirit**. Something that always amazes me about decluttering is that I lose weight, without effort. Decluttering,

minimizing, and streamlining does something to me on a physiological level and helps me let go of weight. I don't try to eat differently but I do forget about snacking, which seems almost like a miracle to me. And when I stop decluttering I feel heavier in myself. But I don't even care that much about the weight, as in, it's not top of mind for me. It's nice to feel slimmer without trying to, *for sure*, but it's not my main focus. It just feels so good to reduce inventory. I feel lighter (in my mind), and it shows on my body. I wonder if how light or heavy we feel in ourselves also registers on the scale? I bet it does.

36. **Look at your home with new eyes**. Sometimes we can become immune to what is around us. So, go out your front door and come back in as if you were a guest. Check out the entrance way. Walk down the hall. Go into your bedroom and bathroom and see if it pleases you. What can you tidy up, move somewhere else or declutter? What hotspots flare up again and again? Can you fix them once and for all? Perhaps with a basket for the junk mail? Or putting a pot plant on top of the microwave so it doesn't become a dumping ground for stray pieces of paper? It's fun how coming into your home with fresh eyes can help you find those blind spots and really spiff up the place.

37. **Swap 'clean' with 'cleanse'.** Think about how different 'cleaning your house' sounds to 'cleansing your space'. Doesn't the latter sound more special and saintlier? Like you are creating your own little sanctuary? It gives a dreamy, spiritual quality to your tasks and makes them feel more sacred. In the book 'The Maid' by Nita Prose (which was a great read by the way), the main character knocks on the door of a hotel suite she is about to clean and asks, 'Is now a good time to return your room to a state of perfection?' When you cleanse your space, you get to slow down and notice what you are doing; to methodically work through an area putting it to rights. To return your home to a state of perfection through the act of cleansing.

38. **Find your tidy-home mentors.** They might be someone you know in real life, a book character or an Instagrammer. My mum's neighbour Ann is one of my organizing chic mentors. She knows my mother well and I feel like I know her by extension even though I have only met her a handful of times. I visited her home once and remember the feeling I had when I was there. Where she lives is stylish and welcoming at the same time as being completely organized and decluttered. It felt very peaceful and zen. When I visited her bathroom, I was in wonder at just how neat

and clean everything was. When I said how lovely her home felt, she said she loves decluttering and that she has one completely empty closet because she has streamlined so much there is nothing to put in there! Whenever I feel like my home is messy and needs straightening up, I conjure Ann's essence and we set to work gladly.

39. **Match clutter categories to life categories**. When you think about your home, where are the perpetually cluttered areas, or which categories rebound back to messy again quickly? *Do they correspond to you as a person*? If the kitchen is cluttered, do you have resistance to cooking at home and prefer to eat out? If your closet is overflowing, do you love shopping for new clothes too often? This is what I found for me: an area that was cluttered meant I was disabling myself in that category. When I committed to tidying up that area, I cured the consequence. So, when I cleaned out my kitchen, my desire for junky food fell away. When I tided and streamlined my wardrobe, online shopping for clothes naturally lessened. I remember when I was writing my first book *Thirty Chic Days*, I kept putting off finishing it. When I look back now, it was because my writing space which was also our spare bedroom was used as a storage space and things kept getting put in there. When I

clicked to this and tidied and decluttered that room, I was able to think better, and the book was finished and released without angst or drama. Where are these areas for you in your home and life?

40. **The simple three-step method** to make decluttering easy. Firstly, choose an area or category. Let's say you're going to look at your candle stash, or your scarf collection. If you have candles and candle holders, or scarves, stashed around the house, you'll need to gather them all up and lay them out. So that's *step one. Step two* is to choose your absolute favourites and put the winners back in the candle cupboard or scarf drawer. Marvel at how you love every one of them, and see how good they look in their spacious environs. And *step three*? Donate the rest. If you aren't *quite* at 'donate', put all the ones that aren't your favourites into a box and put that box out of the way. Look at them later. Are they inspiring to you? Exciting? Or if the box disappeared tomorrow, would you not notice, or even feel *relief*. Try this method on one category and enjoy the simplicity of it!

41. **Maintain your home**. Even if a big decluttering session is not required, regular maintenance is necessary to keep your home feeling good. There will always be a natural

flow of items coming into our house, so we need to ensure that things leave as well. I used to feel like a failure when I had to declutter *again*, because I thought I'd done it properly the first time. It was only when I had the insight that organizing and simplifying is simply good 'hygiene' to be done on a regular basis – much like brushing your teeth or taking a shower – that I felt better about it. Remember, you haven't failed, it's just maintenance. And everyone gets to do it.

42. **'Never leave a room empty handed'**. This very sound piece of advice was drilled into my siblings and me by our mother as children. She did such a good job with her training, that I can never go to a different room at home without checking if there is anything to take with me. Here are a few examples to show you what this means in everyday life. When you get up from the sofa to go to the kitchen, is there an empty coffee cup you can take to the sink at the same time? When you go down the hall to the garage, is there any laundry to drop off to the washing basket in the laundry room which you will pass on the way? And if you are going to your bedroom after dinner, is there any clothing or footwear in the living room that can go with you? You might think this is basic common sense, but not for everyone I have noticed. When you 'never leave a room empty

handed' as habit, tidying up happens effortlessly. Thanks mum!

43. **Gather inspiration to get you off to a good start**. Something I always like to do for a project such as organizing or decluttering, is to start gathering inspiration to boost my enthusiasm. It's like catching a wave into the shore instead of relying on your own swimming horsepower only. Some of my best ways to do this are searching online for decluttered spaces and pinning them on my Pinterest board, reading inspiring decluttering quotes, and revisiting favourite authors such as Peter Walsh and Marie Kondo. Reading the five-star reviews for their books is also a great place to find inspiration. Reviewers are so fired up that their enthusiasm is infectious. Stoking the embers beneath you will pay dividends because instead of thinking 'Urgh, I've GOT to declutter', you'll be more 'Yay, let's start NOW!'

44. **Excuses and reasons that prevent you from starting**. You've been thinking about doing a really thorough and liberating declutter for months, but always put it off for many reasons: *I have other more important things to do, It will take lots of time, I don't have extra time, I don't really have that much clutter, What if I get rid of things I need, What*

if I get rid of too much, But I spent money on it, and so it goes on. You know you are super keen to have a streamlined home that is a joy and pleasure to be in, but it could be a lengthy project and you don't really know where to start. Don't let that stop you though. Honour your desire to live a life of freedom, ease and space. Keep *that* desire in mind: A *streamlined home that is a joy and pleasure to be in, and a life of freedom, ease and space.* Write your vision on a sticky note if it will help. And know you can do it in small pieces of time. Give yourself twenty minutes here, half an hour there, and visualize ahead six or twelve months to see how wonderful life is when you have completed your project. You can do it!

45. **The flip side is pure joy**. When you change the way you think about clearing your clutter, miracles can occur. Instead of looking at it as a burdensome chore that you wish you didn't have to think about, consider this: every book you donate, every piece of clothing you release to find a new owner, and every household item you sell or donate *creates space in your home and your life.* Space in which new energy, activities, hobbies and companionship can enter. When you create this space you will find out what you are excited about *now*, rather than what you found interesting five, ten, or

twenty years ago. *Let yourself clear space. You have nothing to lose.*

46. **100 Things**. Many years ago, I participated in the *100 Things Challenge* and remember it being *so motivating*. As you may have guessed, the challenge is to remove one-hundred items from your home within a set period of time such as one month. The fun part for me was to start a list on a pad of paper, and write things down as I donated (or sold) them. The list wasn't to show anybody, but seeing those numbers and donations stack up really made me want to get to one-hundred. Having a number to aim towards (whether it is 10, 100 or 500) is such a useful motivator; when you look around for things to add to get you up to the number, you will find them! Once you start a list you will see how much energy there is in writing down your progress. And if you find one-hundred a tall mountain to look up to, break it down into chunks and do twenty-five each week. Within a month you will have completed your 100 things challenge and *feel so proud*.

47. **Start with one small area**. If you are frozen with indecision and thoughts of, 'So much to sort! Where do I start?', try this: Choose one cupboard or space and clean it out, leaving only the few things that should be in there.

Make what is left *very attractive* – style and merchandise it for your own pleasure. Note how comforting it is to visit this area every time you use it. See how there are no issues with having to move something to get to another thing and how you gain a little dose of happiness every time you open the door. Then move to another area or room and do the same. You will see how this gradual approach makes such a beautiful difference to your life; how it is to live with functionality and peace. Your home will feel more serene to live in. People will notice you are more relaxed. You will find it easier to care for yourself and others. There is just so much to be gained from having a beautifully ordered home.

48. **You beget what you tolerate**. Clutter builds up gradually. I know this for myself! For some of us it really does multiply when our back is turned for a second. Our home could be functional and easy to maintain and clean, yet it is filled with items we likely will never use again. We stick our head in the sand and ignore certain parts of our home because they are too hard to contemplate sorting. Be inspired by others' efforts – perhaps their home is smaller than yours yet seems more spacious. Take the time to ensure every item you own has a proper place to live, and work

towards lowering your 'inventory' levels so you are no longer shuffling things around.

49. **Curate your wardrobe**. Imagine your ideal closet situation where you would walk in there each morning and love what you see – the items hanging there are like favourite friends. Each piece fits you well and you enjoy wearing it. Wouldn't that be amazing? To get to this point, consider what style essence words resonate with you. If someone asked you to describe your ideal personal style with a handful of words, what would they be? And, do those words match what is in your closet right now? You don't have to change things overnight, but you can lean towards those essence words as you declutter and as you shop in the future. Actually write them down on a little piece of paper and keep it in your wallet, or as a note on your phone. Then, over time, you will indeed look forward to dressing with your ideal wardrobe each day.

50. **Before you buy anything**, jump forward in your mind and ask yourself these questions: *Where will it go? Is there a space already available for it? Just where am I going to store it? How will I feel looking at it every day? Will I get buyer's remorse? Does it fulfil a need or do I just 'want it'? Did I plan to buy this or is it an impulse purchase? Do I already*

have something that does the same job at home that I can use for free? Whether the item is a new side table, a book, or a lipstick, going through these questions will help you be more intentional with what you bring into your home. Yes, it makes shopping less fun, but also, with the things you do buy, you appreciate them so much more because the stress is taken out of the equation. There *is* somewhere for this item to live. It *will* be useful to you. You *will* appreciate it, and you will *not* regret the purchase.

51. **'Just one'**. Keep 'just one' as your motto as you declutter and organize your home, and when you shop for anything new. Just one face cream, not six (use them up and don't buy any more until you get down to the last one). Just one reusable travel cup or drink bottle (handwash it and reuse straight away rather than alternating two). You will spend less and have fewer possessions to store with the *Just One* motto. It will help you resist the urge to stockpile food, buy more magazines when you haven't read the ones you already own, and use up toiletries. It's all free money that is available to you, whether it is saved at the store or 'earned' by using up what you have already purchased.

52. **Create your own daily challenge**. Write down thirty areas in your home you know are disorganized and cluttered, and that if a fairy turned up and waved her wand you would be *so happy* to have them magically transformed. Don't write down big areas, this technique is for the small spaces – one cupboard, a drawer or a storage bin. Each day, choose one item from your list and deal with it. Even if you don't feel like it and even if you're tired. Your daily challenges should take you less than fifteen minutes. Surely you have that to invest for your future serenity? You will be able to effortlessly fill a donation box to drop off, and reacquaint yourself with items you didn't realize you had. At the end of one month you will have all these pockets of beauty and order to lift you up!

53. **Kitchen utensils** inexplicably multiply in my utensil drawer, and I love to use Peter Walsh's simple-yet-extremely-effective method to prune them down. Peter advises to get yourself a box and empty all your utensils into it. Keep that container in your kitchen temporarily, and as you need something, take it from the box. Once the item has been used and washed, put it back into your utensil drawer. After a month, look at what is left in the box and consider if you need to own these things at all. There may be a few seasonal items or less

frequently used gadgets (I love my lemon zester) but for the most part, you probably don't use these items because you have another, newer, favourite duplicate. Perhaps you could donate what's in that box and enjoy your newly streamlined utensil drawer?

54. **Do the same with your kitchen cabinets** if you have the space. Take everything out and store them somewhere else, giving small appliances a good clean if necessary. Pretend you are moving house – pack everything into open-top boxes or place them on towels on the floor and store them in another room nearby. Items will have to 'earn' their way back into your kitchen. You will find that in less than a week your trips to retrieve items you need has lessened considerably. As you put used items back into kitchen cupboards you may find new, easier to access spaces for them too. And then, after a month or so, look at what hasn't moved. Will you ever use these things? Could you get by without them? This technique is a great way to get an instant win with your spacious and newly decluttered cabinets from day one!

55. **Know where your head is at**. For some, doing a complete sweep of their house *a la* Marie Kondo is the best way. And there is also wisdom in slowing the process if you are not

mentally all the way there yet. You will know for yourself how fast you want to go, and your speed may vary over the course of your project too. There will be times when you quantum leap ahead with your results, and times when you want to take your foot off the gas and let everything settle for a while. Both are valid.

56. **Creativity loves flow**. It doesn't matter whether your creativity is writing a book like me, knitting, sewing or crafting, scrapbooking, baking, gardening or cooking a meal for dinner. But when your home is too cluttered and you have to dodge obstacles constantly, both large and small, your creativity is stifled. Your muse will sulk and you won't 'feel like' doing what you normally love to do. Help your muse out by moving (or removing) items that constantly get in the way. Look around at the room you are in right now and these things will instantly stand out. Deal with one and feel the energy shift. Deal with ten and you're making big changes. It doesn't even have to mean getting rid of things either; simply putting items in their rightful place and tidying areas all help your muse too.

57. **Make a list of all the different ways you can rehome items** you no longer need. In my situation this would look like: offering items to others, donating to thrift stores,

selling at our local auction house, and using things up. This will help you be happy to let items go, because you know where they will end up. When we don't take the time to think this through, we can sometimes hang onto things just because we don't know what to do with them and don't want to waste them. Depending on where you live and what you are willing to do, there are other methods too: selling online or at consignment stores, donating to specific charities such as blankets and towels to the SPCA or items useful in setting up a home to the Women's Refuge.

58. **Declutter your own items only!** You can inspire other household members by your example, but you won't be popular if you try to railroad them into doing the same as you, no matter how excited you might be about your newfound passion for decluttering. I know, it's hard when you see an area of mess that you are itching to go through! My husband's top drawer in his bedside cabinet barely shuts because he puts all his detritus in there after work each day, but do I touch it? No! I did jokingly say once that if he wants to give me the best birthday gift, he could let me clean out his top drawer but that's the only time I've mentioned it. Talk about a test of my patience! But I remember that patience is a virtue so I hold my tongue, and let him have his drawer

of rubbish. (And I'm sure I'm not so perfect either!)

59. **Resist stockpiling**, no matter how good the deal. This is how we end up with too much in the first place. There will always be special offers. You won't miss out, I promise. I used to be someone who stocked up on supermarket specials and yes, I did save money, but I think I save just as much money now by keeping a smaller stock of food on hand and shopping weekly. Plus, I no longer have to fit all the excess into my kitchen and make sure I'm keeping up with what needs to be eaten before it goes stale. It is a far more relaxing way to live.

60. **Create your own limits**. Perhaps you will choose a certain number of clothes hangers that feels like the right number for you. Or designate a certain amount of shelf space for the books you want to keep in your personal home library. You'll keep a basket in the pantry for herbs, spices and packet mixes. Then, once your chosen area can't hold any more, you know you've reached your limit. You will either have to use up what you have, or declutter if you want to add more. As Dawn from 'The Minimal Mom' on YouTube says, 'Make the boundaries the bad guy, not you.' (Dawn is my favourite decluttering and minimal living

YouTuber. If you haven't met her yet you're in for a treat!)

61. **Keep things in one place**. All your spare light bulbs in one storage container. Towels on one shelf. All bar soaps in one basket. Same with winter socks. This seems so rudimentary, but you might find, as I did, that once you start organizing different parts of your home you find multiple storage areas for the same item. Decluttering and organizing your home is such a great way to 'find' cash (sometimes even literally) because you don't need to shop for certain items for *quite some time*. Especially so with consumable items such as stockpiled food or toiletry items, but also for clothing and household linens. When you realize just how much you have, you get to enjoy what you already own rather than go shopping for more.

62. **Be 'ruthless' in your own way**. We all have a personal level of how far we're willing to go when it comes to getting rid of things, but perhaps you could push your limits *just a little more*. Keep 'When in doubt, throw it out' or 'Doubt means out' as your decluttering motto. Write it on a sticky note if you need reminding. Doubt means out! When you're dithering, deliberating, or procrastinating, it means you need to declutter that item. Put it into a box and put that box in a cooling off area. I promise

when you come back to it later on, the energetic link will be broken and you'll be happy to see the back of it.

63. **The home detox**. There is a school of thought that your environment reflects your physical being, which I tend to agree with. How else could it feel so good to have decluttered a space? So, if your home is clogged up with extra, unneeded items, is your body also clogged up? Would you do well to identify anything that doesn't serve a purpose and 'flush' it out of your home? Instead of a physical detox, which can be expensive and uncomfortable (I've done a few before), first start on a home detox and you may find that 'everything' loosens up as if by a miracle!

64. **Make over your least favourite place**. A great Feng Shui tip I read was to 'make your least favourite place into your favourite place'. At the time I first read this, the least favourite place in our home was definitely the home office, because even though I wanted to sew and write in there, it had become a dumping ground of items to donate or store and it wasn't a very inspiring place to be. No more though; as I streamlined and cleaned, and scented my home office with a beautiful candle, it became the place I wanted it to be – somewhere that lifts me up and makes me feel

creative and abundant. If I did this same exercise today, it would be my garage. It's never too cluttered, but I haven't tidied it up in awhile and it needs a good sweep. It won't take me that long, so guess what I'm going to do today? I'm actually excited for it! What area of your home would you say is your least favourite, and... just what are you going to do about it?

65. **Go back to wardrobe basics**. It seems crazy that we would have to consider even the most fundamental reasons for having something take up space in our closet, but we do. I know I can still get caught up in the tangle that makes me house items *I don't even like* instead of releasing them to go to someone who will love, wear, and appreciate them. These days, the four standards any clothing item must pass for me whether it's a pair of socks or my best going out outfit are: 1. Do I like this style to look at? 2. Is it physically comfortable to wear? 3. Does it fit and flatter my body shape well? 4. Does it fit my lifestyle and all the things I do? Yes, they are obvious questions, but sometimes we can forget the basics, so I am here to remind you of them as it pertains to your wardrobe.

66. **Everything in your house**... you're only renting it. I heard this concept many years ago

and it helped unravel a lot of stuff in my head about what to keep and what to give away. Nothing we pay money for is ever truly 'owned', and even if we do keep it for a long time, it's not the item that we want, it's what it does for us. We want a comfortable bed for a good night's sleep. We want a new outfit so we can feel confident at a social occasion. As a child I loved my colouring-in books and cut-out doll for the creative play. Holding onto possessions doesn't give us any more of what we've had from it if there is nothing left to give. If the outfit is shabby or no longer fits us, there is no confidence to be had because we can't wear it. If a toy is too young for a child they won't get any value from it. Part of the reason why I love borrowing books and magazines from the library is that I get to return them on the due date. It's the best solution for someone like myself who has a hard time parting with reading material. So, I transferred this idea to things I've bought. Those two matching pillow covers that were $12 each and I've loved in the past but they now no longer go with my bedroom décor? I get to donate them with a free mind because I've told myself I was only renting them for a short while.

67. **When you are considering an impulse purchase**, remember why you are putting the brakes on. Remember how good it feels to be

rid of clutter and how much your savings are growing by not buying more than you need. Put down that item you are contemplating purchasing and see how much lighter you feel – this is instant decluttering and you don't even need to have spent the money! Remind yourself of how much less stress you have in the areas of your life that are decluttered and organized. Advertisers no longer have control over your wallet and they don't get to tell you what to buy. It feels so good!

68. **Not everything needs to be on display**. Part of the serenity of a minimalist home is the peaceful vista of a room. You can look around and your eyes aren't catching on lots of items. Sometimes things are left out just because they are left out. Consider a coffee table which might have a couple of remote controls, a magazine, coasters, and many other useful items. A cleared off coffee table looks so much better. To achieve this pleasing look but still have everything to hand, I found the solution in a medium-sized woven basket which tucks under our coffee table. In this basket are the remotes and coasters, handcream, lip balm and a nail file, a cat brush and a few cat toys. They are all things that are used regularly but don't look good on display. At the end of the evening it is so satisfying to toss everything

back into the basket and have a clean, clear coffee table ready to greet us in the morning.

69. **Return anything borrowed**. Even though I don't consider myself much of a borrower, I found quite a few things in our home that weren't mine. A handful of DVDs of my sister's, and a laser hair removal machine I borrowed from a friend and thought I'd do my own legs with (I found out how long it takes to do even one session and gave the machine back pronto!) There were also a few books and magazines that I'd either read or didn't want to read that could be returned to my mother and aunt, and the library too. Returning items can be considered decluttering because they are still items sitting around unused. What do you have in *your* home that belongs to someone else?

70. **Think what else you could do with the space**. We have a room off our garage which is quite spacious, and carpeted (although not insulated). I claimed it as a sewing room, and of course, what does a room like this attract? Stuff! A lot of stuff! Everything that we couldn't decide where it should go, went in there. It became so full and of course this makes it a rather unappealing place to spend time, so I rarely did any sewing in my sewing room. Then one day we decided to purchase a

treadmill, and with that the incentive came to empty out this room. Fast forward to today, and it's a beautiful clear space with a desk and sewing machine, a treadmill – with a television on the wall in front of it! Such luxury! – and a cube bookshelf with neatly stacked boxes and items that go there. Think about the cluttery spaces in your home. Could you potentially claim a lovely area just by decluttering that space? Imagine a yoga/Pilates/stretching room where you get to leave your mat set up permanently. Or a reading nook with an armchair and a small table. See the potential in your home.

71. **Calm your frugal self**. Your 'clear surfaces' side says 'Get rid of it'. Your thrifty side says, 'But you might need it, and then you'll have to buy it again'. I have found that a small percentage of items I have donated to charity stores, the latter *is* true. But not for the most part. In all my years of streamlining and maintaining possessions, I can remember only one or two items I wish I hadn't donated. And I'm almost certain that if they magically came back to me, I'd donate them again because they weren't as good as I remembered. Remember this when you start having an illogical panic about donating your decluttering efforts.

72. **Be inspired by the extreme minimalists**.
I remember reading about a local couple who
got rid of almost 900 personal items in thirty
days. They gave themselves a month-long
challenge to simplify their life after being
inspired by minimalism. They sold or donated
everything they had collected at the end of that
month. As the month went on they said it
became easier, and they started to feel better
getting rid of something than keeping it. They
also said their home now feels more peaceful
and has less 'noise'. Like me, you might not
want to go as far as them, but gee, those stories
are always so motivating, aren't they? They
light a fire under me and make me want to grab
a box and fill it! You too?

73. **Choose your way**. There is no right or wrong
way to approach decluttering. In my view, the
only wrong way is to never do it and let the
level of your possessions rise in your home
until you can no longer see out of the windows.
But even then, you get to choose. You have free
will. You can choose to fill your house up if you
want to. And, if you want to create more space
you can choose to declutter five items a day, or
spend ten minutes a day scouting for things to
remove from your home. You can choose to
sell or donate, or a mix of both. You can choose
to sell, donate or use up consumables. You can
choose to go room by room, or by categories.

You can have a month-long blitz or go slow over a year. You might have overwhelmed yourself by reading *all the decluttering books*, so sit back and think to yourself, *What feels best to me*? When I ask that of myself, I'd choose to do one drawer, or one room. We are all different in what suits us best so find *your* path of least resistance.

74. **Upgrade to first-class**. Imagine having this as your decluttering filter; when you're going through your closet checking each item to see if it is 'first-class' enough for you. A top that you adore with a tiny hole in the front? If it can be mended invisibly and you can do that? Sure. A top that has gone yellow around the collar and can't be whitened no matter what you try? Out. Or thinking about making a particular room such as your bathroom 'first-class'. You would go through all your products and throw out anything that has become too old, but apart from that you'd tidy your drawers and cupboards, give everything a good clean and revel in your first-class bathroom. Upgrade your car by cleaning it out and keeping it 'empty'. Upgrading to first-class just has such a lovely luxurious ring to it, and effortlessly changes your mindset around decluttering from depriving yourself if you get rid of something, to feeling deprived if you keep it!

75. **Visualize the recipient**. Something that is very helpful if you are finding it hard to let go of items even though you know you aren't getting any use or enjoyment from them, is to imagine you know who they are going to. If I am putting clothes into a donation box it feels good to visualize someone being thrilled to find these pieces at a thrift store. Several years ago I was browsing through the books at a charity store and a man with a baby in a stroller was trying on a suit. He said to the sales assistant, 'What do you think? It's for a job interview'. She agreed that the suit fit him well. When I told my husband about the man in his charity store interview suit that evening, he was so touched that he went straight to his closet. He pulled out all the suits and work clothing he no longer wore, so that someone else could use them for work or a job interview. He immediately saw that just because he didn't have use for them anymore didn't mean they were not useful to someone else. Having the visual in his mind of the man in the charity store made it effortless for him to declutter his closet of clothing he no longer required.

76. **Cultivate serenity**. The more you edit your home, the calmer you will feel. Getting rid of excess baggage means you will end up with your best and most favourite things from every stage of your life. Take out anything that isn't

exactly what you want. Create a place you love to come home to. Be both discerning and disciplined and learn to differentiate between sentiment ('a thought, opinion, or idea based on a feeling about a situation, or a way of thinking about something'), and sentimentality ('exaggerated and self-indulgent tenderness, sadness, or nostalgia'). Liberate yourself by casting aside anything extraneous. Free your mind from excess and infuse your life with serenity.

77. **Receive back ten-fold**. Make a deal with yourself that you will receive back far more than you have removed from your home. It might be ten-fold, or double the amount you donate. Pick a number and know that you will receive this so you can let go with ease. Of course it's impossible to quantify, but imagine if it was true? And the only way to find out was to trust it? You may receive unexpected money or gifts; I have certainly heard many inspiring stories. And if you don't, you will still win. The feeling of peace you'll receive after simplifying your home is worth its weight in gold.

78. **Marie Kondo said,** 'A home free of clutter is a home filled with light'. I have found this to be true, in many definitions of the word light: I feel lighter in my spirit when I have tidied an area or room. I don't feel so bogged down, and

this lighter feeling carries over into other areas of my life as well. My thinking is lighter, my mental state is more buoyant. When you tidy a room and really get stuck in, you can almost feel like you're floating as you walk. It's fantastic! You're just so happy with what you have done. The energy around you is different – fresh, airy and clean. And of course, there are many instances where people lose weight once they have decluttered their home. Why not try it?

79. **Live in a holiday rental**. Coming home from vacation is such a great time to get a new perspective. You've been staying in a hotel, serviced apartment or Airbnb with only a select portion of your belongings with you – your nicest things. It feels elegant and simple to live like this. Holiday accommodation is easy to live in, and there can be a stark contrast when you return home full of exciting plans. You are happy to be back but where did all this... stuff... come from? Are you happy to see everything? Or could you use this homecoming to kickstart an inspiring project to make your home as appealing and luxurious as a vacation rental or five-star hotel by simplifying and organizing?

80. **Create your own minimalism manifesto**. My idea of a minimalist has

always been a free spirit who travels the world with only six items of clothing and a fancy Apple laptop in their backpack. I don't know why, it's just the image that pops into my head. But that can't be the only way to consider ourselves a minimalist. There are as many definitions as there are people in the world. Create your own definition of minimalism to help guide you to your own personal happiness. Mine is that I have just the right number of possessions to help me live my happiest life. I keep books and creative supplies, but a curated and manageable amount. I love to be surrounded by inspiration but can feel when it tips over into too much. I love the phrase 'cozy minimalism' for how I like to live. What belongs on *your* manifesto?

81. **Find your good cause**. Some of us hang onto things because we are afraid they might be wasted. We are keeping them 'safe' but at what cost? At the cost of peace and our sanity, that's what. So scope out where items can go, beyond the usual thrift store donation. Extra collars, leashes, pet clothing and pet beds to the SPCA, mini hotel toiletries to a homeless shelter. Wool and yarn to fund-raising volunteer knitters. Hobby supplies to schools and kindergartens to use for creative work. You really can find a home for anything that is in good condition that you no longer have use

for. I even found a large-scale charity store that had a huge selection of curtains hanging neatly on clothes hangers. I was so excited by this that I went home straight away and dropped back some curtains we had taken down. They were too good to throw away, but I didn't know where they could be donated to; now I did, and it was wonderful to move them along to their next life.

82. **Play the 30-Day Minimalism Game**. I've heard of this but never tried, so I thought I would while writing this book. It's good! Starting on the first of the month, you declutter the corresponding number of items for each day. On the first day you find one item to declutter, on the second, two items and so on. As you progress through the month and build your decluttering muscle, you get up to twenty, twenty-one, twenty-two items per day etc. There is something about hitting that number each day which frees up your over-analytical mind. It's magic is all I can say. Try it for yourself! (The rules of the game say items must be out of your house by the end of that day, but I'm collecting mine in boxes and will donate at the end of the month. This way feels better for me because I can then be 'ruthless' each day, and I also trust myself that I will definitely donate those boxes.) To read more,

search online for '30-day minimalism game' or go to the theminimalists.com/game.

83.   **Create your own theme**. I have always loved the phrase 'a simple life'. It just sounds so peaceful and beautiful, and keeping it as a kind of decluttering mantra helps me clarify the serene vision I desire for my home life to be. It informs what I keep or give away, as well as the colour palette and details such as lighting a candle and putting on soft background music. What could your theme be? Simply creative? Lusciously clean? Peacefully natural? Play around with favourite words that give you good feelings and come up with a fun theme to inspire you to *keep on going*.

84.   **Declutter your hanging clothes** with Peter Walsh's genius reverse-hanger trick. Go into your closet right now and turn all the hangers the 'wrong' way, where the hanger hooks towards you instead of the more natural way. Then, when you wear something and return it to your closet, hang it up the normal way. It will be illuminating at the end of, say, a month, or perhaps the season, *what you have not worn at all*. But why? Was there never the right occasion to wear it? Does it not fit you well? Is it unflattering? Scratchy? Uncomfortable? A not-great colour on you?

Whatever the reason, let the fact that this item is taking up valuable real estate in your closet and offering nothing in return lead you to consider letting it go to someone else who will enjoy wearing it.

85. **Unsubscribe**. Over the past few years I've have been quite zealous in guarding what comes into my Inbox. I belong to barely any email lists anymore, and if I do sign up to one I invariably unsubscribe soon after because I just don't want the 'noise'. The few subscriptions I have kept add value to my life. Even if I 'think' I like that person or company's message but never want to open their emails, I drop the pressure on myself and unsubscribe. I can still read that person's book or visit a store online if I want to. And, when an email from a list does come in, I'm happy to see it and will read it that day. I encourage you to do this too – even if it's an email from me. I only want to be in your Inbox if you're thrilled to see me! You will find that your Inbox won't be shouting at you every time you open it, plus you can't be swayed by special offer emails which could derail your home decluttering efforts. It's incredible how often some businesses send mail. You might be different; you might love all the contact. But if you find it subtly stressful, unsubscribe. Feel the peace. You can always sign up again if you want to!

86. **Look at all you have to gain**. One of my
favourite techniques to make changes in my
life, is to look at all I have to gain with that
change, instead of everything I think I'm
giving up. When I am finding it hard to change
a habit, even though that habit is making me
unhappy, I make a list of both. And in an
instant, I can't wait to get moving forward on
my new habit rather than vacillating between
the old and the new me. So, in the case of
decluttering our home, we consider the money
spent on items we're just going to get rid of,
how long it will take to declutter, how hard it
will be, how annoying to have to clear all this
stuff out, how to sell it if we want to get some
money back, where to throw it away, who to
give it to and so on. Gosh, I feel exhausted just
writing that, and disinclined to do *anything*.
Now, let's look at all we're gaining. A spacious
home with plenty of light, air, and space to
breathe. A sparkling clean environment
because there is less to clean and take care of.
The chance to downsize our home in the future
without stress. Being surrounded by all of our
favourite things and nothing that brings us
down. Not feeling embarrassed when people
call in unannounced. Feeling good in ourselves
because we have followed our desire to have a
beautiful, decluttered, easy-to-live-in home.
Doesn't these outcomes sound wonderful? Do

it for yourself and make a big list of *everything you have to gain*.

87. **Your dream home in a year**. From today, look twelve months out. Now, take a little indulgent time to close your eyes and imagine that date next year. See how lovely your home looks; it's like a chic boutique hotel! See how happy everyone is who lives there. They're living their best life. Go for a walk around and open up the closet doors, peek into the bathroom and take a look through the kitchen. Everything is so neat and orderly. Any drawer you open is streamlined, tidy, and easy to close again. In the linen closet fluffy towels are stacked neatly. It really is your dream home. And yours could be like this in real life. You can get a lot done in a year so why not draw up a fun plan? Choose twelve areas to focus on and do one a month: you could make the first month your bedroom, second month your kitchen etc. Or approach things in a different way, perhaps by category and break it down into small sections once a week or every two weeks. Whatever you choose, look forward to that date twelve months ahead with a feeling of happy elation. The time will pass anyway, so why not make it count? Chat with your future self and listen to her pep talks. 'You can do it!' she says, 'Let's make it fun! We're working towards *our dream home*!'

88. **Live in a celebrity home**. I love those tabloid magazine articles where they show you through a celebrity's home. Have you noticed in these spreads that the celebrity always sits on their kitchen counter for a photo? Always! You don't have to do that, but you can if you want. It would be a fun thing actually, when you have decluttered your home, or at least your kitchen, you could tag me on social media with your 'I'm a celebrity and I'm sitting on my kitchen counter!' photo. Anyway, consider yourself to be a celebrity, because you are in your own life. And your home is the place you will be showing the photographer around when they want to do a feature on *you*. Consider how they'll see it when they come in. What areas will they take photos of? When I think of this, being a celebrity author (obviously!) they will want to take photos of my office. So I will be decluttering, organizing and cleaning it before they arrive. And the rest of the house too because I am a pillar in the community! Being a celebrity means you must have consistently high standards because there are always people looking at you. You don't want people thinking you're a slob. It's such a fun motivator to clean up your home!

89. **Decide what you want to keep**. Marie Kondo says rather than decide what you want to get rid of, decide what you want to keep. I

am in this camp too. It's so freeing, and goes with my own personally successful way of decluttering, which is to take *everything* out of a space: dishes from the kitchen, clothes out of the closet, or books off a shelf. Then, put back only your favourites and the ones you are excited to see. Look at what's left and consider – seriously – if you really want to keep them. It is a technique *exquisite in its simplicity*.

90. **A gift is not a whole-life thing**. When you think about it, a gift's reason for being is to convey a sense of love or gratitude from one person to another. What it is *not* meant to do is bring a layer of guilt, resentment or be a burden to the giftee. I enjoy giving someone a gift, but would be horrified if it caused the receiver emotional angst over what to do with it if they didn't use it. I would prefer them to do with it whatever made them happy. And it is the same for us. Once someone gives us something, it is ours. We no longer need to tie it to them. We get to use that gift and enjoy it, then move it along if we want to. A gift's job was done *at the time of giving*. Cut the cords and take full ownership of all gifts you have been given. Practice with something small and see how it feels!

91. **It's okay to want a different life** from the one you have. Don't let yourself get to the end

of your life and look back with disappointment because you weren't able to do what you wanted to. If you desire to live in a free and lightweight way, do what it takes to achieve that. If you have always wanted to 'throw everything out', why not? If those minimal home images and descriptions tug at your heart strings, make a start. It may take days, weeks or even months of decluttering and distributing, but *you* get to live the life you want. It's your life. Choose yourself.

92. **'Order comes from location'**. Think about how your home would best function and you're likely to come up with some form of this phrase. It is closely related to the saying, 'A place for everything and everything in its place'. As you declutter, reconsider the best location to house items you've kept. It sounds so simplistic, but when you lower your inventory, things get to be easy. You get to move freely around your home and live in it in a relaxed manner, yet everything still gets done. 'Order comes from location'. So simple!

93. **Clearing your space can change your life**. You have to start before you get to feel the benefits, but thankfully you don't have to wait right until the end. When you choose one thing to declutter or one space to cleanse, the feel-good begins. When you do the minimalism

game and declutter 1 thing on the first day, 2 things on the second day etc, at first you start out thinking it's pointless, but as you go through the days of the month you realize you're starting to feel amazing. Shifts are happening. You are upgrading other areas in your life without even trying to. The benefits are cumulative and you only need... to start.

94. **Move with the times**. Back in the day, I used to love magazines. Love, love, love them. I spent a lot of money but gained a lot of value from them so I'm definitely not complaining. I read, re-read, and referenced my beloved magazines. I even based my identity on my favourites at the time, and tore many pages out for my inspiration files. Then, I realized I wasn't into magazines so much. Books inspired me more, and of course more and more images have moved online with Instagram and Pinterest among others. But I still had my magazines surrounding me. It's been a process to let them go, and I have done this in stages. I can't see myself having 'none'; I have my favourite 'Victoria' magazine, many issues are vintage, but who knows what the future will hold even for them? All I know is, I'm moving with the times, indulging in nostalgia yes, but also looking forward. I have a great quote by the late magazine editor Franca Sozzani saved, which really says it all:

'If you're stuck in the past, beholden to it, then your creativity is stuck there too, because you don't give yourself a chance to evolve.' It's ironic that this was said by a magazine editor! But also a push for those of us who are magazine-lovers to move with the times.

95. **Items are not memories**. At one point I realized that some items around me weren't bringing me joy even though I was keeping them for their 'memories'. Some of those memories weren't so easy but I kept the item anyway! On an old episode of *Oprah*, I remember Peter Walsh saying to someone, 'This clock is not your grandfather', which has stayed with me to this day. We believe we have to hold onto a physical item to remember someone by, but do we? It depends if we like the item for its own merits or if we are just keeping it to hold onto a loved one who has departed. After my dad died four years ago, I kept a handful of items that I love, such as his Macdonald tartan kilt, and I have them on display. The kilt hangs on the wall in our living room and suits our décor style. I love that it is both a memory and beautiful. You will know what memory items you need to move on because they will give you a little 'twinge' of emotional discomfort when you see them. Life is too short to live with uncomfortable twinges!

96. **Become the style editor of your home**.
Just like being your own personal stylist can
help you clean your closet (as explained in
Chapter 5. Your own personal stylist, in my
book *How to be Chic in the Summer*), so too
can being your own home style editor. Look at
your home through fresh eyes – the chief style
editor's eyes! Ask your client – you – what
kinds of things she imagines herself enjoying
doing in her home, how she wants to feel there,
and what her favourite colours, styles and
fashion eras are. Then, go through your home
together and brainstorm little tweaks to move
your home in this direction. As you go, I'm
sure your home stylist will point out areas that
would be a lot easier and more pleasurable to
live in once they are simplified – any home
improvement makeover always starts with
clearing out the excess. I hope you enjoy your
session with your stylist and get a lot out of it!

97. **Gather inspiring images** in a Pinterest
folder; fill it with whatever inspires you to keep
on going with your decluttering and
organizing. For me, it's 'empty' spaces –
beautifully staged minimalist rooms, clean
and brightly lit orderly fridges colourful with
fresh produce, and elegantly curated closets –
especially closet advertisements! Build up
your folder over time and come back to it when
you need to remember why you're doing this.

Add other images too, of your goals. Maybe a resort vacation, being your ideal weight, or having paid off debt. Cleaning out your home of items that no longer represent you will help towards all your goals. I love the saying 'a rising tide lifts all boats', and it's applicable here too. When you feel successful in one area, you'll find it easier to be successful in another.

98. **Always have a box handy**. Something that has helped me keep my decluttering maintenance going is to keep a donation box nearby at all times. I store mine in a room off our garage, and whenever I come across something and think, 'I'm sick of looking at this and never know what to do with it', I march it straight to the donation box. The box isn't going that day, so it's an easy way to detach from the object without fear of making a wrong decision. And when I come to deliver that box to a thrift store, 999 times out of 1,000 I don't want to retrieve anything from the box. It's an excellent system for painless decluttering.

99. **The benefits of decluttering**. When you need a reminder, come back to this tip and be blown away by all the incredible benefits of living in a decluttered home. It's a wonderful list! When you declutter, you have less to clean, less stress in your life looking for lost

items, less to pay for, less debt, less to look after, less to insure, less to tidy away, less to organize, less dust and grime to build up, less low-level anxiety, less burdensome feelings, more peace of mind, better sleep, more tranquility, higher productivity, boundless creativity, more energy and enthusiasm for everyday living, improved mental health, more ability to be mindful and live in the present moment, more time to yourself, and you get to live in a more spacious home that is easy to clean and care for. Phew! Are you persuaded yet? Ready to get back into your decluttering?

100. **Claim your dream life**. This is your one life. You owe no explanations to anyone else, even those closest to you. If you are bogged down with things you are looking after for other people, give them back with a smile and say you are tidying up. Start creating your dream life by emptying it of things that don't bring you happiness and filling it with things that do. This will look different for everyone, so allow yourself to brainstorm and dream just what your ideal life looks and feels like. What kinds of things will you do? How will you dress? What do you surround yourself with? What is your desired décor look and how can you achieve this starting where you are? I am drawn to images of extremely minimal rooms – they just seem so peaceful to me. But I love

to live a cozy, creative life. Cozy minimalism is probably the closest thing to my style, but **every style** is helped by clearing out the excess. It's worth doing. You're worth spending time and energy on. You will *gain* more time and energy when you go through the process of tidying and curating your home. It's a worthy goal and I promise you will feel happier than you ever have before. It's just a natural by-product of cleaning up your environment. Have fun creating your dream life!

50 Extra Tips to Declutter Your Home in a Happy, Positive and Easy Manner

Here we are at the end! I do hope this book has helped you find more pleasure in your home, and that you have been effortlessly pottering around getting rid of things all over the place! It's so much better when you get to achieve your goals from a place of being pulled along by your excitement rather than trying to push yourself. It takes less energy, you get more done, and most crucially, you enjoy yourself more. Before you know it, you'll be one of those people on Instagram showing off their newly decluttered guest room.

To give you a little bit more oomph before I send you out into the real world (or more likely, down the hall to your garage to get started), here are fifty extra little tips of goodness to inspire you to declutter your home in a cheerful and enthusiastic state of mind!

1. Take an optimistic approach to decluttering your home; know that this project is going to be the making of you, your home, and your relationships.

2. Don't be overwhelmed by all that you have to do. Even if you only remove a handful of items today, you will still be further along than yesterday. Imagine if you decluttered five items a day for a month, that's 150 items! Or 1,825 if you can keep doing that for a year!

3. Treat your possessions with respect and appreciation, whether you are decluttering or keeping them.

4. Have the goal of keeping the right number of possessions for you and your space.

5. Declutter a category *before* you buy any organizing tools for it. You may find you don't need anything extra.

6. Keep your systems simple. This becomes easier once your inventory levels are lower, but even to begin with you can 'choose simple'. You don't need a complicated decluttering system; you can start to make progress with one idea from this book.

7. Declutter your clothes rather than buy extra hangers. You will have tons of hangers left!

Then, keep only your favourite, matching hangers and declutter the rest.

8. Do small things as you see them – take a cup to the kitchen, file an invoice, hang up a top. It's easy to train yourself into this and you will find your home stays tidier without effort – like it's the fairies doing it!

9. Use it or lose it. If you come across something you 'know' you'll want to use one day and that's why you've always kept it, give yourself a deadline to do just that. One week is a reasonable time frame, but if one month feels safer, give yourself a month. Sometimes even just choosing this option helps me declutter something without regret that I was sure I needed.

10. Brian Tracy says that you feel good about yourself and happy with life in general to the extent that you feel in control of your surroundings, and I agree. It's a fabulous feeling. Gaining control over your home will empower you in so many ways.

11. If you work better with a guide, there are plenty of decluttering checklists available when you search online, or create your own by listing out the areas you know are an issue for you and have fun checking them off one by one.

12. Approach your home like you are inspecting it for a job. You are a decluttering consultant hired by the lady of the house. See every area with fresh eyes and write down what you see on a list held by a clipboard. A clipboard gives you instant credibility as a decluttering consultant!

13. Join an online decluttering challenge if this sounds fun to you. There are so many! Simply search for 'decluttering challenge' and choose one that appeals.

14. When tidying an area, set your timer and see how much you can get done in ten minutes. I am always amazed at how far my time goes when I do this.

15. Choose your top three areas of stress and start with those categories. Instead of your home being a source of anxiety, know that you can create a place of *rest and comfort* by decluttering. What are three areas in your home that cause tension for you?

16. Take *Before* and *After* photos. The great thing about a Before photo apart from having a satisfying comparison, is that often you don't see what is right in front of you – taking a Before photo gives you a fresh perspective. If you're already half-way through an area before you

remember, still take a photo. You will see a pleasing difference between the two.

17. Gain momentum by doing something every day. Print off a calendar page (they're easily found online, or use a calendar you already have) and tick off each day that you've decluttered something.

18. Dream of your beautiful future where you are living in a perfectly staged show-home. Close your eyes before you go to sleep and visualize your rooms. Drink in the serene spaces. Do this every night and call your dream home towards you as you do the practical decluttering by day.

19. Remember how good it feels – you do actually feel lighter! – to not stuff your life full, to have space to *breathe* and *feel free*.

20. Include social plans and obligations in your decluttering – are there regular events you go to that you just don't want to do anymore? Exit them gradually and gracefully.

21. Remember Dave Ramsey's quote to 'live like no-one else today so you can live like no-one else tomorrow'. Write it down somewhere to keep your encouragement up for living the way you do and cultivating your own 'chic minimalist' mindset.

22. Find out what you need to be happy. For me, I'm a real home-lover and relish time spent in my abode surrounded by the things I love such as books, music, and creative projects. Trim the excess around you and really let your main passions take centre stage.

23. Become someone who is intentional with what they allow into their life, whether it is an item, an obligation, or a person.

24. Create a guiding theme for your decluttering. Mine is *A Simple Life*. What will yours be?

25. Commit to using things up before you buy more, in all categories: stationery, crafting supplies, food, cosmetics and toiletries, baking supplies, and candles. There are so many areas in which we can find ourselves overstocked, and we can just as easily let inventory lower over time when we temporarily stop purchasing in that category.

26. Collect different sized boxes before you start so you can get instant gratification filling them. Write on the sides where each box is to go, or just consider that 'all cardboard boxes are for donation'.

27. Stop shopping while you declutter. You don't need the distraction of items coming in. Become obsessed with decluttering instead of spending!

Start a list of items you genuinely do need and fill in those gaps as a reward at the end.

28. Read and discard your magazine stash a few at a time. Sometimes it's just a quick flick to confirm there is nothing you need in this magazine, and sometimes you'll take a photo of a recipe or tear an inspiration page out.

29. Become someone who enjoys doing the laundry because they love everything they've worn and washed, and there is plenty of room to put it away when it is clean, dry, and folded.

30. Sort through your inspiration files (such as printed out articles and magazine pages). You will find some real gems in there once you weed out those which are no longer relevant to you.

31. Be honest with yourself if selling discarded items is really an option. For many of us, the energy spent as well as the small financial gain means it is preferable to donate.

32. If you have a Tupperware-type collection, get rid of anything that doesn't have a matching lid, and also containers you just don't like using. I prefer mine to be see-through otherwise I forget about things in the fridge. If I can't see it, that leftover lunch option doesn't exist!

33. Consider how many pens, rubber bands, bread bag ties and paper clips you really need. Keep a handful in a small container and donate or throw out the rest.

34. Be willing to repurchase in the future. We can't guess everything we might need one day, and it doesn't feel good to keep *all the things* just in case. So allow yourself to live for the current season in your life *and* give yourself the option to buy anything you might need in the future. Your peace of mind is worth a possible future purchase.

35. You may be shocked to find you have so much 'stuff' when you thought you were a streamlined kind of person. Me too! But that's okay. At least we're doing something about it now. Many people are like us, but only a few intentionally declutter. Be one of the few.

36. If you were to die tomorrow, would you be embarrassed at everything you've left behind for someone else to clean up? Let that light a fire under you – imagine your loved ones doing the job you are doing now!

37. Once your home is in a decluttered state that you are happy with, implement a maintenance check every month, where you find ten things to declutter, or spend half an hour going around

your house scanning for hotspots which may have popped up.

38. Find motivation where you can. Sometimes a hoarding programme does this for me. Watching a video of a lady who stored 75 tonnes of items in her 3000 square foot house was scary enough to make me want to stay on the straight and narrow.

39. Instead of feeling like you are sacrificing by getting rid of so much stuff, feel liberated. Feel *free*. Think of all you are gaining: a serene home, more space, and a more relaxed, carefree lifestyle.

40. Have a goal for your home. My goal is for ours to be like a boutique hotel. Stylish, warm, friendly, and charming, and neat, organized, and spacious too. It's a delightful place to stay!

41. Run your home *like* a hotel. Have simple, effective systems in place and aim to always be on top of things. Be that smartly dressed maid creating order wherever she goes.

42. Run your books through the library test. Would you get this book out of the library for free? If the answer is no, it's a little depressing to think of the wasted money but freeing at the same time. It is so easy to sort books once you apply the 'Would I check this out for free?' question.

43. Think 'luxury vacation rental' when tidying and decluttering your home. As in, *How can I create a beautifully relaxed vacation feeling for myself every day of my life?* And, *Does 'this' belong in my luxury holiday home?*

44. Play your favourite music while you go. Sometimes I'm in the mood for upbeat top 40, sometimes classical strings, and sometimes relaxing piano or spa music. Music makes decluttering more enjoyable, and the time goes faster.

45. Ask yourself: *If I were to move to a brand-new house tomorrow, would I take this item with me?* People tend to get rid of a lot of stuff when they move because they like to start over. Why not give yourself this freedom today?

46. Everything in your home has potential, for sure, and some of us are great at seeing the potential in *everything*. But do we want to see all those things through? Do we have the bandwidth for that? Get real about where you see yourself going and decide from that place. Ask yourself honestly if you really want to finish a DIY project (or start one).

47. If you have spending regret, redirect it to, 'Okay, lesson learned, let's move on'. Get out of your emotions and be efficient and practical instead.

And, give yourself as much grace as you'd give someone else.

48. Know that once an item is out of your house, you are highly unlikely to think about it *ever again*. Instead, you'll be appreciating your simplified life with a calm and clear mind.

49. When we lighten the load on our home, it's not only going to be a more enjoyable place to be, but we get to feel excited about going into the next season of our life. We are traveling light and feeling flexible. We can move, change, and go where we need to go. We are no longer weighed down by extra, unnecessary possessions.

50. Find magic in everything you do *so you can live a magical life*. This is what it all comes down to. We are decluttering our home so we can live our most beautiful, serene, and happy life. Find enjoyment in the process as well as the outcome. Take pleasure in every minute of your decluttering time. Make it a cheerful experience and approach your simplifying with confidence, joy, and delight.

So, what are you going to do next? Which tip is nipping at you to try right now? Harness your enthusiasm and do even one small thing straight away. Or open your notebook and jot down some ideas and fun plans. Write down a blueprint of your ideal life, how wonderful your home will be 'when', and how you plan to get there. Note down exciting words that zing you up. Pump up your volume!

I am truly excited for the transformation that is to come for you, your home, your relationships, and your happiness. Even while writing this book, I was decluttering more than usual while I wrote the tips and ideas. I was the one coming up with the content and it still effortlessly motivated me! I cleaned up some 'sticky' areas for me such as magazines and I couldn't be happier about it.

I wish the same success for you and would love to hear how you get on. The very best way, and the one that means the most to me, is to leave a review on Amazon. It's the best compliment you can give to an author. I would be so, so grateful if you could take a few minutes to leave a review to update me with your decluttering and simplifying wins.

And, if you'd like to be notified about my new releases, click the Follow button on my Amazon author page here:

amazon.com/author/fionaferris

Wishing you all the best in your decluttering journey. May it be easy and fun, and you achieve incredible, life-changing results!

Fiona

About the Author

Fiona Ferris is passionate about the topic of living well, in particular that a simple and beautiful life can be achieved without spending a lot of money.

Her books are currently published in five languages: English, Spanish, Russian, Lithuanian and Vietnamese.

Fiona lives in the beautiful and sunny wine region of Hawke's Bay, New Zealand, with her husband, Paul, their rescue cats Jessica and Nina and rescue dogs Daphne and Chloe.

You can find Fiona's other books at: *amazon.com/author/fionaferris*

Other books by Fiona Ferris

Thirty Chic Days: *Practical inspiration for a beautiful life*

Thirty More Chic Days: *Creating an inspired mindset for a magical life*

Thirty Chic Days Vol. 3*: Nurturing a happy relationship, staying youthful, being your best self, and having a ton of fun at the same time*

Thirty Slim Days: *Create your slender and healthy life in a fun and enjoyable way*

Financially Chic: *Live a luxurious life on a budget, learn to love managing money, and grow your wealth*

How to be Chic in the Winter: *Living slim, happy and stylish during the cold season*

How to be Chic in the Summer: *Living well, keeping your cool and dressing stylishly when it's warm outside*

A Chic and Simple Christmas: *Celebrate the holiday season with ease and grace*

The Original 30 Chic Days Blog Series: *Be inspired by the online series that started it all*

30 Chic Days at Home: *Self-care tips for when you have to stay at home, or any other time when life is challenging*

The Chic Author: *Create your dream career and lifestyle, writing and self-publishing non-fiction books*

The Chic Closet: *Inspired ideas to develop your personal style, fall in love with your wardrobe, and bring back the joy in dressing yourself*

The Peaceful Life: *Slowing down, choosing happiness, nurturing your feminine self, and finding sanctuary in your home*

Loving Your Epic Small Life: *Thriving in your own style, being happy at home, and the art of exquisite self-care*

The Glam Life: *Uplevel everything in a fun way using glamour as your filter to the world*

100 Ways *to Live a Luxurious Life on a Budget*

100 Ways *to Live a European Inspired Life*

Printed in Great Britain
by Amazon

47619742R00057